Contents

A Star Reborn   Andrew Lloyd Webber

'leave me, leave me, 'tis a great pity if a man cannot take a glass of wine by his own fireside'

Thus spoke RIchard Brinsley Sheridan when he was disturbed at a Covent Garden café while watching his Theatre Royal Drury Lane go up in smoke on 24 February 1809.

The building that disappeared in a blaze so bright that it interrupted Parliament at Westminster was the third theatre on the site. The present theatre is the fourth, although it was extensively remodelled in 1922, when the auditorium was completely rebuilt.

Happily, although shamefully mistreated, the superb Greek Revival front of house designed by Benjamin Wyatt to replace Sheridan's pile of cinders did not succumb to the wrecker's ball. However, the ugly new auditorium looked more like a cinema than a theatre, whereas Sir Nikolaus Pevsner wrote that the Greek Revival front of house 'is unmatched anywhere in London'.

I remember the late Robert Nesbitt, the legendary producer of the Royal Variety Performance, lecturing me early in my career. 'The London Palladium and Drury Lane have the same number of seats. When there's half an audience in The Palladium it's half full. In The Lane it's half empty.' Famously the 1922 auditorium was once described as 'An important example of The Early Hideous Period'.

The task of restoring the Theatre Royal was threefold: how to reinstate Wyatt's glorious 'front of house' rooms, how to fix the 1922 auditorium and how to make this extraordinary building a versatile, vibrant heart of the artistic soul of Covent Garden.

The huge project needed different skills. Theatre architects Haworth Tompkins were appointed in overall charge, with specific responsibility for the stage and auditorium. Dr Simon Thurley was appointed chairman of our steering group and has been my right-hand man on all matters architectural and historical.

Mindful of Robert Nesbitt's structures, the auditorium has been completely remodelled. The stage has been brought forward to incorporate two former side boxes. The Royal Circle has been extended forward and the back wall of the stalls brought forward by 20ft. The seating capacity has been reduced from 2,250 to 1,900 to greatly improve sight lines and leg room. Access to the Stalls, which previously involved going down the Rotunda staircase, snaking tortuously through corridors only to climb up yet more stairs to the auditorium, is now at street level as Wyatt intended.

Wyatt's two identical staircases were created so that King George III, who had fallen out with his son the Prince of Wales, could enter the theatre with their respective hangers-on without bumping into each other. Thus the Theatre Royal Is the only theatre with two identical staircases and two royal boxes. As a nod to history, every seat in the audltorium on the King's Side is embroidered with a crown and on the Prince's Side they sport the Prince of Wales's feathers.

The decoration of the superb Rotunda and the staircases posed a conundrum. Analysis of layers of paintwork revealed that there had been more than a dozen decorative schemes since 1812. So clearly nobody was ever happy with them. After much debate, Simon Thurley and I decided on a colour scheme taken from the recent redecoration of the staircase at Woodhall Park in Hertfordshire. I hope that over two hundred years later, it finally is right.

Another conundrum was the huge niches on the staircases. They are too shallow for pictures, but obviously were meant for something. We wondered if they were intended for grisaille work that was never carried out because Sheridan went bankrupt. So grisaille artist Ian Cairnie was commissioned to create eight canvases. Two grisailles on the lower levels depict putti playing various

The auditorium during and after restoration.

roles in shows that have been in the theatre. On the upper level the vast canvases are tributes to two groundbreaking shows that played here. On the King's Side are scenes from *My Fair Lady* (1958). On the Prince's Side, two depict scenes from *Show Boat* (1928), which, of course, was the first musical to tackle racial inequality. The third is a fanciful scene of my hero, composer Richard Rodgers of Rodgers and Hammerstein fame, playing for some of his leading actors. Starting with *Oklahoma!*, Rodgers and Hammerstein had four of their most famous musicals play The Lane. Oscar Hammerstein II also wrote the book and lyrics for *Show Boat*.

All this has been a joy to restore and create, but the most important work was obviously to make the theatre itself fit for the 21st century. Thrillingly, it is now possible to stage a production at The Lane completely in the round. To achieve this, the front of the Royal Circle can be removed so the Circle meets a floor that covers the Stalls and joins the stage to the auditorium. Banks of purpose-built seats complete the job. Theatre in the round can be achieved in 48 hours.

On a technical level, the rebuilt fly-tower now has a grid that can take the weight of 18 double-decker buses. Underneath the enormous stage is a 40ft-deep void, so scenery can appear from below. I believe that The Lane is now one of London's most warm and beautiful auditoriums and the most versatile historic theatrical space anywhere in the world.

Before the 1922 remodelling, the Theatre Royal was hugely associated with productions of Shakespeare plays. After 1922 Shakespeare was rarely performed here. The last production was *The Tempest* in 1957 directed by Peter Brook with Sir John Gielgud as Prospero. I was lucky enough to be taken to see it. In fact, it might have been my first taste of theatre — it was either that or Norman Wisdom as Aladdin in *The Wonderful Lamp* at The London Palladium.

The newly refurbished Rotunda: a champagne bar and a statue of William Shakespeare.

9

Installing the new seating, with more legroom and better sightlines.

OPPOSITE Maria Kreyn's paintings of scenes from Shakespeare's plays provide a striking contrast to the austere classical architecture of the great stairs.

Memorably on the last night of *The Tempest* Sir John broke Prospero's staff and proclaimed that the Theatre Royal was lost to Shakespeare and henceforth would only play American musicals. Despite the profound impression the next show, *My Fair Lady*, made on me, I am determined to prove Sir John wrong and one day have a Shakespeare season in the theatre.

While we are waiting, and audiences are lapping up *Frozen The Musical*, visitors will find the statue of Shakespeare by John Cheere in pole position as they enter the Rotunda.

I am particularly thrilled by the eight paintings I commissioned from the Russian artist Maria Kreyn based on the essence of eight Shakespeare plays. These are hung at the bottom of the two staircases from the Rotunda. Both Maria and I are hugely grateful to Sir Trevor Nunn for his insight into the plays we chose.

The restoration of the Theatre Royal has been a colossal task rendered very difficult by the Covid pandemic. It simply would have ground to a halt without the dedication of our extraordinary craftsmen and the team overseeing the project in at times almost impossible circumstances.

At times we wondered what more could be thrown at us. Only two months before opening, all the bespoke furniture for the front of house that was waiting to be installed was lost in a warehouse fire – but luckily all the mahogany carpentry we had commissioned for the front of house was in place. It is by Mark Stephens and comes from St Nicholas's Abbey in Barbados, where several magnificent trees were lost in a storm a decade ago. It is typical of the resilience of our brilliant project manager Dan Watkins that somehow it has all been remade. I owe Dan a huge vote of thanks.

Finally, my biggest debt is to my wife Madeleine. A few years ago she embraced this enormous project and has never wavered in driving it through and taking the lead during some very testing times. Without her support this restoration would not have happened.

Madeleine and I hope that the Theatre Royal will become a vital part of the Covent Garden community. We want to welcome you all through its doors all day and every day for everything from cocktails to coffees and lots, lots more.

Timeline

1663	Killigrew's theatre opens with a production of *The Humorous Lieutenant*.
1665	Nell Gwyn makes her debut as an actress.
1672	First theatre burns down.
1674	Second theatre, attributed to Christopher Wren, opens.
1687	World's first theatre playbill is printed at Drury Lane.
1702	First British pantomime is staged.
1742	David Garrick, 'the first modern superstar', makes his first appearance.
1745	First performance of 'God Save the King'.
1791	Second theatre demolished.
1794	The third theatre opens, the largest of the four, seating 3,600.
1796	The Baddeley Cake ceremony, the world's oldest theatrical tradition, begins.
1800	Assassination attempt on King George III by a disgruntled ex-soldier.
1809	Third theatre destroyed by fire.

1812	Fourth, and current, theatre opens.
1813	Drury Lane becomes the only theatre in the world to have two royal boxes.
1817	Drury Lane becomes the first theatre in Britain to be lit by gas.
1847	The body of the ghost of the Man in Grey is discovered bricked up in a wall.
1889	Sir Augustus Harris introduces modern pantomime.
1894	Substage machinery installed allowing the stage to be raised and lowered.
1909	Running of the 2,000 Guineas with 12 live horses in *The Whip*.
1916	Frank Benson becomes the only actor ever to be knighted in a theatre.
1925	The era of the musical begins with *Rose-Marie*, *Desert Song* and *Show Boat*.
1958	*My Fair Lady* opens, starring Julie Andrews and Rex Harrison.
1989	*Miss Saigon* opens, to become the theatre's longest-running production with 4,263 performances over ten years.
2000	Andrew Lloyd Webber acquires Drury Lane.
2021	Following LW Theatres' £60m restoration, the stunning theatre opens.

Killigrew's Theatre Charles II and the first Theatre Royal

Banned during the puritanical Commonwealth (1649–60) because of its association with disorder and sexual licence, theatre was seen as one of the symbols of the Restoration and when Charles II returned to London in 1660 after more than a decade in exile, the reopening of playhouses was eagerly anticipated by all classes of society.

The new King granted Thomas Killigrew, a fellow royalist exile, permission to set up one of 'two houses or theatres for the representation of tragydies, comedyies, playes, operas, and all other entertainments of that nature'. Until this time, female roles had always been played by young men and boys, but Charles II had seen an actress while in France and his royal charter stipulated that in his new theatres 'all the women's parts shall be played by women'. The first British actress is thought to have been Margaret Hughes, who began her acting career in 1660.

Killigrew leased a parcel of land between Drury Lane and Catherine Street. Hemmed in by properties on all sides, the plot was far from ideal, with access limited to two narrow passages, each 10ft wide, one from Catherine Street and the other from Drury Lane, but there was room to build a theatre that seated 400. Samuel Pepys thought it was 'made with extraordinary contrivance', while another visitor wrote that it was 'the most proper and beautiful that I have ever seen'. It would have fitted on the stage of today's theatre.

The first theatre opened on 17 May 1663. In addition to the main show of the day, there were other performances of drama, dance and music that ran on late into the night, lit by hundreds of candles. There were few rehearsals

Thomas Killigrew, sometimes known as the 'Pimpmaster General', painted by William Sheppard, 1650.

Nell Gwyn

Nell Gwyn started her career selling oranges at Drury Lane. Noted for her bawdy humour on and off the stage, she made her debut as an actress at the theatre in 1665 and fast became a favourite with the audiences. Today Nell is most famous as mistress to Charles II but at the time she was much admired for her talent as a comic actress.

In the auditorium, too, the atmosphere could be chaotic, with comings and goings between — and during — the various performances. On benches in the pit sat a motley assortment of young gentlemen, some ladies 'of Reputation and Vertue' and a good many 'Damsels that hunt for Prey', few of whom paid much attention to the drama on stage. An observer in 1698 described how they sat all together 'higgledy-piggledy, chatter, toy, play, hear, hear not'. The press of bodies created a stench so overpowering that many playgoers bought oranges sold outside the theatre to sweeten their breath and counteract the smell during the performance.

The first theatre survived London's Great Fire of 1666 but was destroyed in 1672 when a fire started 'under the stairs where Orange Moll keeps her fruit'. Undeterred, Killigrew built a new theatre, possibly designed by Christopher Wren. More grand and much larger than the original, the second theatre on the site seated 2,000 and was the first to have an entrance on Drury Lane itself. It was opened in March 1674 in the presence of Charles II.

and the performers were hampered by the men who sat on the stage to ogle the female actors and who made an equal nuisance of themselves backstage, where actresses allowed favoured gentlemen to watch them dress and where money bought other intimacies. Before long the theatre's reputation for scandalous behaviour was firmly re-established.

Shakespeare at Drury Lane

Shakespeare's plays have been performed at Drury Lane throughout its 350-year history but it was David Garrick in the 18th century who was responsible for rekindling an interest in Shakespearean drama, restoring the original texts in performance after many years of cutting and adaptation by actors.

Some of history's finest actors were famous for the great Shakespearean roles they played on the stage at Drury Lane. Audiences in 1740 flocked to see Charles Macklin's interpretation of Shylock in *The Merchant of Venice*. Until then Shylock had been played as a comic character, but Macklin gave the role such ferocity and power that a terrified George II was unable to sleep after watching the performance.

ABOVE LEFT Edmund Kean (1787–1833) was a celebrated Shakespearean actor whose first performance as Shylock at The Lane gave rise to the expression 'an overnight success'. His statue is now alongside that of Shakespeare in the Rotunda champagne bar (right).

ABOVE RIGHT John Gielgud as Prospero, *The Tempest* (1957).

Henry V (1938) with Ivor Novello. Novello dominated the British stage in the 1930s.

Sarah Siddons was a great tragedian whose most famous role at Drury Lane was as Lady Macbeth in 1785. She is credited with being the first actor to invent the stage business of washing the imaginary blood from her hands. Edmund Kean was another Shakespearean actor who made his reputation in 1814 playing Shylock as an evil monster in a black wig. The meagre audience was so impressed by this unknown's performance that word spread during the interval and the theatre was crammed for the second half, leading newspapers to coin the phrase 'an overnight success'.

The fourth – and current – theatre on the site opened in 1812 with a production of *Hamlet*, starring R.W. Elliston.

Shakespeare's tercentenary in 1916 was celebrated at Drury Lane with a performance of excerpts from all his plays, including Frank Benson as Julius Caesar. Immediately after the performance Benson was summoned to the Royal Retiring Room to receive a knighthood from King George V. Other Shakespeare productions at the theatre in the 20th century featured some of the leading actors of the day, including Edith Evans in *A Midsummer Night's Dream* (1924), Ivor Novello as *Henry V* (1938) and John Gielgud as Prospero in Peter Brook's production of *The Tempest* (1957). Gielgud broke his staff at the end of the last night of the run to symbolise the end of Shakespeare at The Lane, leaving the theatre to become the national home of the musical.

Maria Kreyn's Shakespeare works

At the foot of the stairs are eight paintings by Maria Kreyn, a Russian-born American painter who works in a traditional style but with an intensely emotional contemporary vision. Commissioned by Andrew Lloyd Webber in 2019, these paintings of some of Shakespeare's greatest plays – *King Lear*, *Othello*, *Romeo and Juliet*, *Macbeth*, *As You Like It* (below left), *A Midsummer Night's Dream*, *Hamlet* and *The Tempest* (above left) – capture the emotional intensity of each play's major themes rather than representing actual scenes, and reinforce the Bard's long association with Drury Lane in a new and powerful way.

Garrick's Theatre An acting revolution

Often described as 'the first modern superstar', David Garrick was one of Britain's greatest actor-managers, dominating the English stage for 30 years and leaving a legacy of reform and dramatic practice that continues to influence the theatre today.

Garrick began his theatrical career as a playwright and made his first appearance on the stage at Drury Lane in 1742. He had been a student of Charles Macklin, a colourful character who once stormed off stage and felled the prompter with a blow before returning to explain to the audience that 'the scoundrel prompted me in the middle of my Grand Pause'. It was Macklin who pioneered a naturalistic style of acting, one that would seem stilted and stylised to audiences today but that was seen as excitingly new at a time when the fashion was for actors to strike a pose and declaim their lines in a formal manner. Garrick revolutionised this approach, popularising an ever more natural way of speaking and moving on stage. A versatile and daring actor, Garrick brought an unprecedented realism to the parts he played. He transformed theatrical practice in other ways too, scrapping inherited parts, where the costume, gestures and business of a particular role were handed down intact from generation to generation. Instead, he insisted on proper rehearsals and would fine actors who failed to attend. It was Garrick, too, who rejuvenated interest in Shakespearean drama and restored the original endings of the tragedies.

Famous for his intense energy – George III described him as 'a great fidget who could never stand still' – Garrick took over the management of Drury Lane in 1747. Under his direction, the theatre enjoyed three decades of

David Garrick as Richard III, painted by William Hogarth.

commercial and artistic success during which the reputation of the stage was transformed.

When Garrick first joined Drury Lane, playhouses were as popular and as disorderly as they had been in the 17th century. Theatres provided entertainment for all classes of society and attempts to raise revenue by increasing ticket prices or abolishing half-price admission after the third act, as Garrick tried to do in 1762, were met with sometimes violent protests. Drury Lane and other theatres were often the subject of complaints for being 'full of prophane, irreverent, lewd, indecent and immoral expressions', and it was common for plays to be disrupted by the comings and goings of the audience. Garrick attempted to tackle the problem by enlarging the first gallery and making patrons pay on entry to the boxes, and he banned the practice of sitting on the stage and paying for the privilege of going backstage to watch

LEFT David Garrick by Sir Joshua Reynolds. Garrick's influence on theatre was so great that he was given a state funeral on his death in 1779.

BELOW The theatre in Garrick's time, built in 1674. It was demolished by Richard Brinsley Sheridan in 1791.

actresses dress – or provide other services – often during the performance itself.

The changes Garrick instituted at Drury Lane were soon followed by other theatres in Britain and elsewhere. His influence on theatrical practice was profound and long-lasting. Not only did he radically alter acting techniques, he also established ideas about appropriate costuming and the use of special effects using scenery, props and lighting, which transformed theatres around the world from social events to places of enthralling drama.

Murder at Drury Lane

The Green Room at Drury Lane was the scene of a murder in 1735, when Charles Macklin stabbed a fellow actor in the eye with a stick during an argument about a wig and then attempted to help by urinating on the wound. He conducted his own defence at his trial for murder and managed to reduce the charge to manslaughter, although he was never jailed and the case had little effect on his popularity. Macklin continued acting until the age of 93, when he forgot his lines for the first time and turned to the audience: 'Ladies and gentlemen, I have been seized with terror of the mind', he said. 'I am retiring. Goodnight.'

His Majesty The King and Her Majesty The Queen Consort in the Royal Box on the King's Side (during a visit in June 2021 as His Royal Highness The Prince of Wales and Her Royal Highness The Duchess of Cornwall).

A Royal Theatre

The theatre in Drury Lane has always lived up to its name with its many royal associations. Since 1663 every reigning British monarch has visited theatres on the site, and previous sovereigns also enjoyed a night at The Lane. Charles II, of course, was a frequent visitor, with Nell Gwyn, one of its first actresses, perhaps the most famous of his many mistresses.

The current theatre is unique in having not one but two royal boxes. Before the old theatre burned down in 1809 there were royal fisticuffs there when George III encountered his eldest son and heir, later George IV, who was drunk at the time. Both were keen playgoers, but on that occasion the King was so enraged by the sight of his dissolute son that he set upon the Prince and boxed his ears soundly. The scene was said to have caused so much embarrassment to those watching that steps were taken to separate them In the new theatre, giving the royal pair separate entrances and separate boxes, on opposite sides of the auditorium. The story continues to be celebrated in the new restoration, with the two sides of the theatre divided into the King's Side and the Prince's Side, each distinguished with a special monogram for the signage, seats and carpets.

Attempted assassination

On 15 May 1800 George III visited Drury Lane to watch a performance of *She Would and She Wouldn't* in Sheridan's huge and short-lived theatre. The band was playing 'God Save the King' to announce his arrival when an ex-soldier called James Hadfield fired a pistol at the King, narrowly missing him. Hadfield, later judged insane, was secured and George III insisted that the play should go ahead, although the audience was in an uproar, the Queen and princesses in tears and the performers agitated and confused. 'Never was a piece so hurried over', wrote one witness.

The Royal Box on the Prince's Side is decorated with the Prince of Wales's feathers.

Visits from later monarchs were less fraught, although at times just as unusual. In 1916 the actor Frank Benson was summoned to the Royal Retiring Room after his performance as Julius Caesar, to be knighted by King George V. The prop sword initially offered for the ceremony was felt to be 'out of keeping with the solemnity of the occasion' and replaced by a proper sword, hastily acquired from a local military outfitter.

Some monarchs were not above influencing what happened on stage as well as off it. Sarah Siddons's death scene in *The Mysterious Husband* moved George III so much that by royal request the play was never performed again, while Ivor Novello changed the ending of *Careless Rapture* after being told by King George V that the last scene of *Glamorous Night* had made Queen Mary cry.

Drury Lane has hosted the annual Royal Variety Performance on a number of occasions. First held at the Palace Theatre in 1912, the show is attended by members of the Royal Family and features a wide range of acts from the top performers of the day, raising money for the Royal Variety charity in aid of retired entertainers.

The Royal Retiring Room.

OPPOSITE **His Majesty The King (during a visit in June 2021 as His Royal Highness The Prince of Wales) pictured leaving the Royal Box on the King's Side.**

Sheridan's Theatre 'A wilderness of a place'

David Garrick was succeeded as manager in 1778 by Richard Brinsley Sheridan, a playwright notorious for his casual attitude to deadlines, so much so that on the opening night of *Pizarro* he was still writing Act 5 when the actors were on stage performing Act 2. A celebrated wit, MP and leader of fashionable society, Sheridan had little time for the practicalities of financial management and his love of extravagant spectacle nearly bankrupted Drury Lane.

He refurbished the auditorium in 1783, turning it into 'the prettiest and most elegant Theatre that London could ever boast'. Four years later he had the theatre painted white with gilt mouldings and ornaments, only to decide in 1791 that the building constructed in 1674 was too small and antiquated and should be demolished completely.

In 1794 a third theatre opened on the original Drury Lane site. It was a huge building for its time, capable of holding 3,600 people and described by Sarah Siddons, the leading actress of the day, as 'a wilderness of a place'. The new theatre was financed by selling 300 subscriber shares at £500 each. In return they received free admission and 2s 6d (12½ pence) for every performance. While the size of the auditorium was intended to raise badly needed funds for the theatre, the design also incorporated new technologies. The designer, Henry Holland, promised that the new arrangements for the stage 'are upon a larger scale than in any other Theatre in Europe'. The scenery could now be raised, lowered or drawn off to the side by

RIGHT **Richard Brinsley Sheridan painted c.1790 by John Hoppner.**

OPPOSITE **The third theatre on the site had seating for some 3,600 people.**

Anchovy sandwiches

In 1777 the only way the actors could get Sheridan to complete *The Critic* in time for the first performance was to lock him in the Green Room, with a bottle of port and some anchovy sandwiches, until the play was finished.

The fire at the Theatre Royal Drury Lane, seen from Westminster Bridge, 1809.

means of machinery, which avoided the need for scene shifters getting in the way of the performance.

More importantly, the new theatre was designed with a number of fire safety measures. Scenery painters at the time had little choice but to work by candlelight and the combination of flames, paint and wooden boards made the theatre environment highly combustible, while naked flames that provided lighting during the performance were also a continual hazard. The roof of the new theatre contained four large reservoirs of water intended to extinguish fire, although Holland was confident that they should not be needed, especially with the new iron curtain that had been installed to completely separate the auditorium from the stage and thus to prevent the spread of any fire.

The new theatre opened in March 1794 but was not to survive long. Barely 15 years later, on 24 February 1809, a fire broke out shortly after 11pm. Holland's fire precautions had been neglected: there was hardly any water in the reservoirs and the iron curtain had rusted up. The fire ran up the front of the boxes unimpeded and within half an hour the roof had collapsed.

Sheridan was in Parliament at the time but went later to watch the destruction of his theatre from a nearby tavern. 'Leave me,' he is said to have replied to an onlooker, ''tis a great pity if a man cannot take a glass of wine by his own fireside.'

The destruction of the theatre left Sheridan with an enormous debt of £436,971, equivalent to more than £20m in today's money, and Drury Lane with an uncertain future.

The roof of Sheridan's theatre collapsed in the 1809 fire but a new theatre rose in its place. The auditorium ceiling has been restored to its Georgian glory with spectacular plasterwork and gilding.

Backstage Theatrics

Special effects had been used in productions long before Killigrew built his theatre. Wires, trapdoors, ropes and harnesses were all used for dramatic entrances and exits, while fireworks, trumpets, drums and sometimes real cannons created the sounds of battle. Salts and alcohol were burned to create coloured smoke and early actors wore animal bladders filled with blood which would burst and spurt blood convincingly when punctured by a sword.

It was Sheridan who took the public's thirst for spectacle to a new level at Drury Lane. The short-lived third theatre that he built on the site was huge, and he needed to fill seats. Sheridan's solution in 1795 was to put on a play featuring a lake of real water on stage and starring a performing dog called Carlo. Carlo was trained to swim across the lake every night and rescue a little girl from drowning. The audiences went wild and Carlo became a massive star, pulling in the punters and raising much-needed funds for the theatre.

In the 1890s, manager Augustus Harris restored the theatre's fortunes once more by putting on popular sensation dramas. To create new and exciting shows that would pull in the audiences, he set about improving the outdated technical facilities for moving scenery and installed a state-of-the-art stage system under the stage.

The earthquake scene from *The Hope* (1911) and the sea rescue in *Sealed Orders* (1913).

OPPOSITE *The Whip* (1909) featured special effects including a train crash, a replica of Madame Tussaud's Chamber of Horrors and the 2,000 Guineas race run with real horses.

Special effects in *Miss Saigon* (1989–99):
a helicopter appeared to land on the stage.

galleon and a chariot race with 16 real horses. The horses, four to a chariot, were suspended on cradles above treadmills that kept turning under their hooves as they galloped, while the wheels of the chariots were worked by rubber rollers operated by electric motors. An impression of speed was created by a huge panoramic backdrop depicting the arena filled with spectators revolving in the opposite direction.

Just as elaborate was the 1907 production of *The Sins of Society*, which featured a weir disaster by moonlight, the Longchamps Races and the sinking of the troopship SS *Beachy Head*, with soldiers saluting the flag as they met their doom. In 1920 *Garden of Allah* saw the stage transformed into the Sahara Desert, complete with horses, camels, goats and a spectacular sandstorm, much of which ended up in the front stalls on opening night thanks to a technical error. The effects were not enough to prevent the *Daily Telegraph* opining that the play was 'a great deal of high-falutin [*sic*] twaddle', but audiences didn't appear to mind. The more elaborate the sets, the more popular the shows seemed to be.

Stage effects continue to thrill audiences today. Projections are used to create effects, from floating clouds and digital rain to huge moving panoramas, while dry ice can conjure up fog or rivers and two-way and backlit mirrors allow characters to disappear in a flash. In one notable scene in *Miss Saigon*, which had a record-breaking run of 4,263 performances, the helicopter landing was so convincing that some members of the audience asked if they could watch the helicopter arriving from the street!

Audiences were enthralled by the extraordinary spectacles the substage made possible: sinking ships, avalanches and horse races, earthquakes and submarines. *The Sleeping Beauty and the Beast* in 1900 was described as 'an orgy of marvellous mechanical effects and scenic beauties'.

The same could have been said of many spectacular shows of the late 19th and early 20th centuries. The 1902 production of *Ben Hur*, for instance, featured a sinking

Substage machinery

Many of the special effects that made shows so popular in the 19th and early 20th centuries were created by the engineers who operated the complex system of levers and pulleys that controlled the three sections of Drury Lane's famous Substage. This consisted of three independent lift systems, built in three phases. The first, installed in 1894, was a hydraulic system, unique in Britain at the time, which could not only raise and lower the centre stage area but also tilt, rock and scissor it. In 1897, new-fangled electricity was used to put in two upstage lifts, while the two downstage lifts installed in 1930 were also electric.

Wonderful as it was, the old machinery was not usable in the modern theatre for safety-at-work reasons. But now the Substage can be used to create effects that the Victorians could only dream of. Increased mechanisation has made it possible to do away with the scene shifters who were once employed to move heavy pieces of scenery around during a performance. When the theatre was renovated in 2019–21, the question of what to do with the Substage was a contentious one. It formed an important part of theatrical history but the lifts had not been used for some time and the space below the stage was needed to create electronic effects that would thrill and enthral 21st-century audiences just as much as those of the 19th and 20th centuries. The Substage lifts remained in perfect working order to the end. A final performance was given in front of an invited audience of engineers and theatrical historians before the machinery was removed and preserved as a museum exhibit or for use in another theatre.

His Majesty The King and Her Majesty The Queen Consort take afternoon tea with Noel Coward on the Grand Saloon terrace (during their visit to the theatre in 2021 as His Royal Highness The Prince of Wales and Her Royal Highness The Duchess of Cornwall).

OPPOSITE *Cavalcade* had a cast of 400, many of them on stage at the same time.

Cavalcade

Playwright, actor, producer, composer, lyricist, film director, film star and cabaret artist, Noël Coward was one of the greatest theatrical stars of the 20th century. He was noted for his wit and many of his plays have become standards that are still performed.

His most successful collaboration with the Theatre Royal Drury Lane was the 1931 production of *Cavalcade*. A jingoistic but anti-war pageant featuring scenes from the Boer War, Queen Victoria's funeral and a railway station, *Cavalcade* had a cast of 400. There were so many people on stage, in fact, that the weight of the chorus prevented the stage lift from working on the opening night. The production proved immensely popular, the original investment of £30,000 recouping

£300,000 (approximately £14m in today's money).

Cavalcade coincided perfectly with a political crisis. The removal of Great Britain from the Gold Standard led to a burst of patriotism that swept a Conservative National Government to an unprecedented victory at the General Election held two weeks after the opening night. When King George V and Queen Mary saw the play on election night, their visit was publicised to restore confidence in the country. Reflecting on the similarities between the current national situation and the show in his opening-night speech, Coward concluded: 'I hope that this play has made us feel that despite our national troubles it is still a pretty exciting thing to be English.'

A Working Theatre

A tunnel with brickwork said to date back to the first theatre on the site runs underneath the auditorium and is used by actors and crew to cross from side to side during performances. Legend has it that the first backstage teams were sailors who were used to climbing rigging and operating the ropes and pulleys for special effects. Waiting idle and unpaid while their ships were docked in the River Thames, they earned extra money helping out at the theatre and left a legacy of nautical terminology: the backstage team are the crew, lighting is on a rig and scenery in a dock. Even today, winches, pulleys and flying ropes are used by the crew and although many special effects are now computerised, the technical crew, or 'techies', have inherited a number of superstitions from their seagoing predecessors. The first crews were used to raising or lowering the sails according to a system of whistle-codes from the ship's bosun and even today whistling onstage or backstage is considered bad luck in case the tune is misinterpreted and might bring some heavy scenery crashing onto the whistler's head.

While the audience throngs the front-of-house area before a show, the backstage area is just as busy. Everything has to be checked before the curtain goes up. The wardrobe department and the dressers set the costumes; the wigs department dresses and sets the wigs. The company manager decides which understudies are to be used and the electricians check the lighting desk and the lights.

Meanwhile, onstage, stage management ensure that all the props are in order and the set is in place. The crew move everything into position for the start of the show. Fly-pieces and scenic cloths are flown in and out and

Many of the most famous names in British theatrical history have passed through the stage door at The Lane.

LEFT The first stage hands were off-duty sailors who were used to climbing rigging and operating winches and pulleys.

The iconic Red Coats who greet visitors to The Lane wear striking gender-fluid uniforms created by avant-garde designer Charles Jeffrey to mark the reopening of the theatre after its restoration. The uniform, consisting of a frock coat in blood-red tartan, with either matching red trousers or a kilt, incorporates jacket linings inspired by the theatre's Greek Revival architecture, while the metal details on the jackets are intended to deliberately 'disrupt the look'.

the sound department checks every microphone and recorded sound effect.

Thirty-five minutes before curtain-up, the actors get their half-hour call, known as the 'Half'. Stage time is always five minutes ahead of real time. If the show starts at 7.30pm, the 'Quarter' is called at 7.10pm, the 'Five' at 7.20pm and 'Beginners' at 7.25pm, which ensures that actors are not still in their dressing rooms when the curtain goes up.

During the show itself, the stage manager is in charge of the stage while the deputy stage manager normally 'calls' the show. This means standing in the prompt corner with a copy of the script, calling all the lighting, stage-management, fly, sound and crew cues. A big show might have as many as 800 lighting cues alone, so it is a pressurised job. The assistant stage managers have

their own 'plots', in charge of stage-right or stage-left. Throughout the show, the crew will be moving large pieces of set and props. The fly-floor crew raise and lower fly-pieces. Electricians operate the lighting desk and the sound engineer the sound desk, each part of a skilled team without which the spectacular shows so loved by Drury Lane audiences could not go ahead.

The box office

Killigrew's theatre had four entrances where tickets were sold for each show, the money being collected in a small box. Once the performance had started, the four ticket sellers took their boxes into an office inside the theatre and tipped the money into a larger box to be counted together, which eventually gave rise to the term 'the box office'.

Superstitions and Traditions

The Theatre Royal is famous as the most haunted theatre in London, if not the world. Its most famous ghost is the 18th-century figure known as the Man in Grey, sighted on many occasions in the Grand Circle. Unusually, he only appears during the day. Wearing a long grey riding cloak, riding boots, a powdered wig and a three-cornered hat, he has a sword at his side and walks, it is said, from one side of the auditorium to the other, following the line of the building's original seating, before disappearing into a wall very close to where a grisly discovery was made in 1847. Workmen renovating the auditorium knocked through a wall into a void only to find a skeleton with a dagger in its ribs.

The body was reburied properly, but the Man In Grey continues to haunt the theatre, where he has been seen by hundreds of people, including members of staff and matinée audiences.

ABOVE The ghostly figure of the Man in Grey appears in one of Ian Cairnie's grisaille paintings.

OPPOSITE The Lane is one of the most haunted theatres in the world.

Dan Leno, 'The Funniest Man on Earth'

Dan Leno was a 19th-century music hall star who starred in 15 consecutive pantomimes at Drury Lane, where he created the role of pantomime dame and made it his own. Although also a talented actor, it was as a comedian that Leno had his greatest success, and by the time he made his first appearance in America, he was billed as 'the funniest man on earth'.

The entire cast of *Miss Saigon* looked up from their bows at the end of a matinée in 1999 and all saw him at the same time. His appearance is seen as a good omen.

Actors and crew waiting in the tunnel below the auditorium have sometimes reported hearing footsteps passing close by them, while the backstage areas of the theatre are said to be haunted by the ghost of the comedian Dan Leno. A practical joker, Leno suffered from incontinence and drenched his clothes in lavender oil to disguise the smell. There have been many reports of a lingering scent of lavender in the air that cannot be otherwise explained when things go wrong in the theatre.

Charles Macklin is another actor who is reported to visit Drury Lane still, in spite of dying in 1803 at the remarkable age of 107. Macklin was famous for knowing every line of every play and it was claimed that if you forgot your lines, he would tap you on the shoulder and whisper them to you. Even in recent times, actors have reported their minds going blank, only to feel a tap on the shoulder and suddenly remembering their words.

Actors are notoriously superstitious. Most famously, quoting from or even mentioning Shakespeare's *Macbeth* by name is thought to be unlucky. In a theatre, it is always referred to as 'The Scottish Play' instead. If you do mention the title by mistake, the curse can only be broken by exiting the theatre, spinning round three times, spitting, cursing and then knocking on the door to be let back in.

Actors avoid wishing each other 'good luck' before they go on stage too, preferring a more cryptic 'break a leg'. The origin of this phrase is uncertain, but it may refer to the counterweights attached to the curtains at the front of the stage which were known as 'legs'. They were very fragile so if you had turned in a wonderful performance and the audience kept calling you back for more curtain calls, you might cause the 'legs' to break.

Other superstitions include not whistling or having mirrors on stage, never using peacock feathers and ensuring that the last person to exit the theatre at night leaves a 'Ghost Light' on stage.

Julie Andrews (Eliza Doolittle) helps cut the Baddeley Cake for members of the cast of *My Fair Lady* on 6 January 1959.

The Baddeley Cake Ceremony

The world's oldest theatrical tradition, the Baddeley Cake Ceremony that takes place on Twelfth Night (5 or 6 January), dates back to the 18th century. Robert Baddeley was a pastry chef who became an actor and spent most of his career at Drury Lane. When he died he left £100 for 'the purchase of a Twelfth Night Cake or Cakes and wine and punch or both them which... it is my request the Ladies and Gentlemen performers of Drury Lane Theatre ... will do me the favour to accept on twelfth night every year in the Green Room'. The custom has continued to be observed since 1796 at Drury Lane, where the assembled cast drinks a toast to Baddeley. Nowadays the cake is always a homage to the show being staged at the time and the punch is made by the theatre manager from a secret recipe kept under lock and key.

Whitbread's Theatre
Georgian elegance, Victorian spectacle

When the destruction of his theatre left Sheridan facing ruin, he turned to Samuel Whitbread, a distant relative who had made a fortune from brewing, to help clear his crushing debt and save the theatre at Drury Lane. Whitbread, an MP, created a Committee of Renters – from which he wisely excluded the spendthrift Sheridan – to clear the huge debt and raise funds for a new building. The Committee raised £400,000 and commissioned Benjamin Wyatt to design the fourth, and current, theatre. Whitbread worked tirelessly to ensure the success of the new project until his death in 1815.

Work began on the new theatre in October 1811. Designed by Wyatt with characteristic Georgian elegance, it had cantilevered staircases and a spacious and light entrance with pillars. In 1817 The Lane became the first theatre in the world to be fully lit by gas. The interior was remodelled in 1841 and a new auditorium added to the original theatre in the early 1920s. The theatre was restored to its original glory between 2017 and 2020.

Onstage, the 19th century was marked by new kinds of shows, from the invention of modern pantomime by

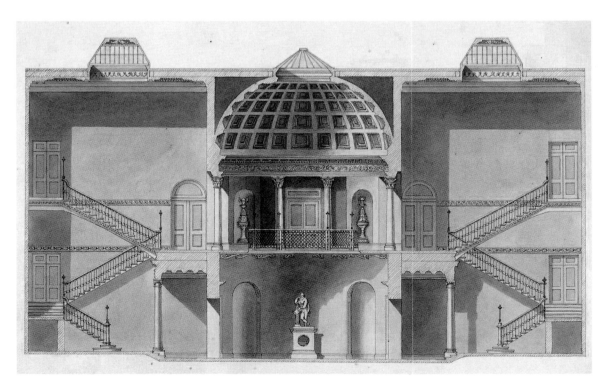

Benjamin Wyatt's architectural drawing showing the cantilevered staircases and the Rotunda that remains at the heart of the theatre today.

OPPOSITE The Rotunda after the restoration.

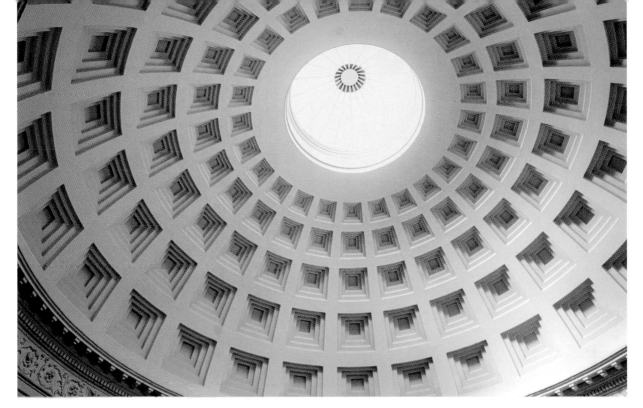

The light and airy Foyer was originally designed as a place for servants to wait with cloaks and outdoor shoes while their masters and mistresses enjoyed the show.

Joey Grimaldi to the first musical. Michael Balfe, who first conducted the orchestra at Drury Lane at the age of 15, became musical director at the theatre and was a prolific writer of opera. Concerned that opera itself was too exclusive, Balfe wrote an operetta to appeal to all classes. *The Bohemian Girl* was first performed at Drury Lane in 1843 and was a huge hit. It is generally considered to be the prototype of the modern musical.

Shows that appealed to popular taste continued to be produced throughout the 19th century, so much so that in 1875 one critic despaired of 'the ignorant

pleasure-seekers who, flocking to Drury Lane, have turned what should be a national theatre into something not widely different from a circus'. While the shows were a hit, management was an ongoing issue. Alfred Bunn (manager 1833–39), described by the *Theatrical Times* as 'the presiding genius of dramatic humbug, the great incarnation of Managerial quackery', was only the first in a series of managers who went bankrupt, absconded with funds or quarrelled, sometimes violently, with the actors.

By the end of the century, however, Augustus Harris led Drury Lane into a period of calm that coincided with some of its greatest success. The size of the stage lent itself to the spectacular melodramas that were so popular at the end of the 19th century. Harris employed the latest machinery, including the theatre's famous substage, to achieve effects that made the audience gasp at such spectacles as an earthquake, a sinking ship and a race with 12 live horses.

Many operas, ballets, dramas and pantomimes were performed at Drury Lane as well as melodramas, but it was musical comedy that took the theatrical world by storm in the 1920s. *Rose-Marie*, the first American musical imported to the theatre in 1925, broke all previous records at Drury Lane, and was followed by *Show Boat* starring Paul Robeson in 1928.

The years that followed saw ever more lavish musical productions that brought audiences flocking to the theatre throughout the 20th century and into the 21st, with iconic shows like *My Fair Lady*, *Oklahoma!*, *Oliver!*, *Miss Saigon* and *42nd Street* firmly establishing The Lane as the home of musicals.

Second World War

During the Second World War the theatre became the headquarters of the Entertainment National Services Association (ENSA) and survived a gas cylinder bomb that ploughed through three levels, tearing the bottom out of the Grand Circle, but fortunately failed to detonate. Members of staff acting as ARP wardens in the theatre to put out incendiary bombs were sleeping in the area but miraculously no one was hurt. The remains of the bomb are on display today in the tunnels beneath the auditorium.

The Home of Pantomime

The first English pantomime, *Tavern Bilkers*, was staged at Drury Lane in 1702, although it was not recognisably the Christmas classic known today. The early pantomimes originated from the Italian *commedia dell'arte*, a partially scripted entertainment with stock storylines and characters, including the zany, crude trickster servant called Arlecchino (Harlequin in English), who performed in mime alongside the clown in the 'Harlequinade'. John Rich, who was briefly the manager of Drury Lane in the early 1700s, often played Harlequin. His routine was to chase the other characters around the stage, slapping them with two sticks joined together at one end and giving rise to the term 'slapstick'.

A century later, Joey Grimaldi was famous for playing Shakespeare's jesters at Drury Lane. He developed the traditional pantomimes, introducing both dialogue and storylines based on fairytales in 1815. In the 1880s Sir Augustus Harris, Drury Lane's famous manager, expanded the genre further. It was Harris who made the pantomime into the family entertainment we know today, with characters such as the Dame and traditional sayings like 'Look behind you!' or 'Oh, no he isn't!' Harris's pantomimes were huge extravaganzas with elaborate sets and live animals, and he introduced music hall performers into the cast for the first time. It was something of a gamble with the respectability of the theatre but it paid off, increasing the sales of pantomime tickets by drawing in audiences from the local music halls. In spite of the fact that they often ran for over six hours, the shows were wildly popular and sell-out performances virtually guaranteed, enabling pantomime to secure the financial future of many British theatres. Tastes change, however, and the last pantomime at Drury Lane took place in 1935.

The 'Grand Xmas Pantomime' in 1900—1 included 'an orgy of marvellous mechanical effects and scenic beauties'.

Mr. GRIMALDI, as Clown.

Grimaldi's costume was copied by later clowns. The close similarities can be seen in this scene from *Sleeping Beauty* (1912).

Grimaldi: The first clown

The world's most famous clown, Joseph Grimaldi, made his stage debut at Drury Lane in 1791 aged three, and went on to transform pantomime by introducing not only the now traditional costume for a clown (white face, red cheeks, tufts of hair and loose breeches) but also many standard routines featuring a string of stolen sausages, pick-pockets, opening an oyster and grasping a red hot poker. The emphasis on verbal comedy and storylines based on nursery rhymes and fairy stories in pantomimes today is also attributed to Grimaldi. He had huge success at Drury Lane and at Sadler's Wells, often running between the two venues to perform at both theatres on the same evening. One contemporary wrote: 'Neither the wise, the proud, the fair, the young, nor the old were ashamed to laugh till tears poured down their cheeks at Joe and his comicalities.' To this day, Grimaldi's grave is visited each year by a conventicle of clowns, who are still known as 'Joeys' in his honour.

Show-Stopping Musicals

The Theatre Royal Drury Lane's reputation as the home of musicals dates back to the 1920s, when *Rose-Marie* was the first American musical to be imported from the US in 1925. It broke all previous records at Drury Lane, and was followed by *Show Boat* starring Paul Robeson in 1928.

The years that followed saw ever more lavish musical productions. While some asked despairingly how long Drury Lane was to be 'the asylum for American inanity', audiences loved the new musicals. During the Second World War the theatre became the headquarters of the Entertainment National Services Association (ENSA). But apart from those few years, Drury Lane has been associated with spectacular musicals ever since, with iconic productions of *Oklahoma!*, *South Pacific*, *Carousel*, *My Fair Lady*, *A Chorus Line*, *Miss Saigon* and *42nd Street*.

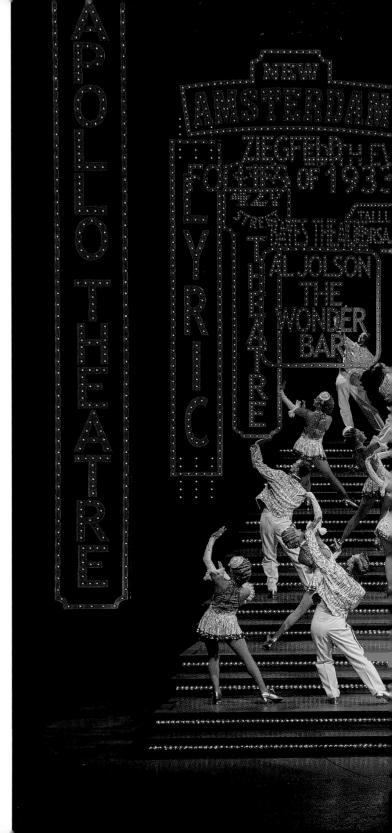

Scene from the spectacular revival production of *42nd Street*, the last show at The Lane before the theatre closed for restoration in 2019.

SHOW BOAT

Unusually for the time, Jerome Kern's *Show Boat* tackled racial issues. The show opened to great acclaim in 1928 and starred Paul Robeson, Edith Day, Cedric Hardwicke and Marie Burke. During the run, Robeson also played to packed houses with afternoon singing recitals.

CARELESS RAPTURE

Ivor Novello dominated the British stage in the 1930s as writer, composer and producer of musicals in which he also starred, notably at Drury Lane. With his matinée-idol good looks, Novello took the leading non-singing roles in lavish productions such as *Glamorous Night* and *Careless Rapture*, which tapped into the public's desire for romance and escapism with a topicality that made them hugely successful at the time, although they are rarely performed nowadays.

OKLAHOMA!

Pulitzer Prize-winning *Oklahoma!* is generally accepted as being one of the most important musicals ever written,

Show Boat (top) opened in 1928. *Oklahoma!* (1947) (above) was a huge hit in post-war Britain. *A Chorus Line* (opposite top) opened in 1976, while *Miss Saigon* (1989–1999) (opposite bottom) is the longest-running show ever at The Lane.

blending as it did dance, drama and music seamlessly together in a ground-breaking format that ensured its instant success in the austere atmosphere of post-war Britain.

CAROUSEL
Carousel (1950) was Oscar Hammerstein's personal favourite of the musicals he wrote with Richard Rodgers.

A CHORUS LINE
Opening in 1976, *A Chorus Line* ran for 1,113 performances. The set was bare compared with previous Drury Lane staging, an empty rehearsal stage backed by a mirrored wall. Jack Tinker commented in his review: 'But as the brilliant simplicity of the concept unfolds tensions fairly clutch the hairs on the back of your neck.'

MISS SAIGON
Miss Saigon ran for ten years from 1989 to 1999 and holds the record of the longest-running show at Drury Lane, with a total of 4,263 performances.

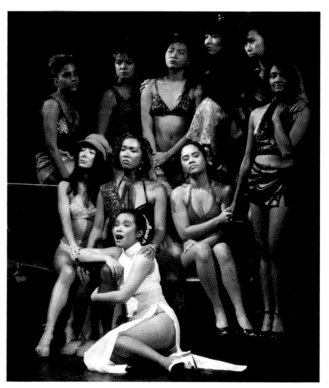

The 81-piece Andrew Lloyd Webber Orchestra rehearses his orchestrated *Symphonic Suites*, with music drawn from *Evita*, *The Phantom of the Opera* and *Sunset Boulevard*, on the Theatre Royal stage, one of the largest in the West End.

OPPOSITE
TOP *The Pirates of Penzance* (1982); *The Producers* (2004); *Hello, Dolly!* (1979).

MIDDLE *42nd Street* (1984); *Sweeney Todd* (1980); *Oliver!* (2009).

BELOW *Dancin'* (1983); *Frozen* (2021); *The Best Little Whorehouse in Texas* (1981).

Rodgers and Hammerstein

Richard Rodgers and Oscar Hammerstein II were one of the most successful partnerships in theatre history. Rodgers composed and Hammerstein wrote the lyrics for *Oklahoma!*, *Carousel*, *South Pacific* and *The King and I*, which played consecutively at Drury Lane between 1947 and 1956. The two men supervised orchestra rehearsals in the Grand Saloon during the last days of rehearsals for all four shows.

Described by the *Sunday Times* as 'one of the best American musicals', Rodgers and Hammerstein's *South Pacific* was based on a Pulitzer Prize-winning novel by James Michener and was a feel-good show, set against a background of warfare, which openly tackled racial issues. It opened on Broadway in 1949, starring Mary Martin, whose portrayal of Nellie Forbush made her a superstar, and was an instant critical and box office success.

When the production moved to Drury Lane in 1951, Martin came too. By the time she left the London production, she had washed her hair on stage more than 3,000 times while singing 'I'm Gonna Wash that Man Right Outa My Hair'.

My Fair Lady

The musical partnership of Alan Jay Lerner and Frederick Loewe was responsible for one of Drury Lane's most successful productions, *My Fair Lady*, which began a record-breaking run of 2,281 performances in 1958. Julie Andrews, Rex Harrison and Stanley Holloway headed the original cast. The scenery was designed by Oliver Smith and the costumes by the Oscar-winning designer Cecil Beaton, after whom the bar in the Foyer is named.

An adaptation of George Bernard Shaw's *Pygmalion*, *My Fair Lady* was a huge hit, with one critic exclaiming: 'the last thing I want to do is drown *My Fair Lady* in fulsome, exaggerated superlatives. It deserves better than that!' Lerner and Loewe's adaptation retained Shaw's wit, he added, and 'where Lerner has added he has done it so well that I am left wondering if I shall ever care again for the original play bereft of his music and lyrics'.

On 7 May 1963 a gala performance of *My Fair Lady* marked both the Theatre Royal's tercentenary and the five-year record set by the show, which closed in October the same year. During its run, 24 members of the cast were married and every member of the Royal Family had seen the show at least once. Margaret Halston, who played the Queen of Transylvania for the entire run, was 83 when it finished.

Julie Andrews and Rex Harrison starred as Eliza Doolittle and Henry Higgins in the record-breaking run of performances of *My Fair Lady* that began in 1958.

The Cecil Beaton Bar serves cocktails such as the 'Beautiful Wasp' and the 'Eliza Doolittle', which are inspired by his work. Some of Beaton's original costume designs hang in the bar.

Cecil Beaton's costumes

Cecil Beaton's costume designs for *My Fair Lady* were vital to the visual success of the production. Beaton drew on his Edwardian childhood to incorporate the fashions he remembered. Julie Andrews later recalled that 'all the clothes were so much more detailed and beautifully made than I'd ever expected'. Beaton's knowledge of the period was, she said, 'extraordinary' and although some adaptations were necessary, 'it wasn't until I had Eliza's shawl on my shoulders and her silly broken hat on my head that I knew how I was supposed to act'.

Lloyd Webber's Theatre

A theatre transformed

The Lane was acquired by Andrew Lloyd Webber in 2000. For some years the theatre continued to be home to many successful musical shows such as *Miss Saigon* or *42nd Street*, but in 2017 Lloyd Webber decided the time had come to restore it, providing all the facilities audiences now expect without compromising the important historic interiors. A £60m project remodelled the stage house with the latest in production technology, re-fashioned the auditorium to provide better sightlines and more comfort and transformed the front of house with new bars and circulation spaces. The majestic Regency Foyer was cleared of accretions inserted in the 1920s and the great staircases opened up to soar upwards to the grand tier once more. The Grand Saloon and former coffee rooms were transformed into comfortable and stylish bars. Care was taken to replicate light fittings and paint colours in authentic Regency style while the theatre's famous collection of paintings and statues was added to by new commissions. The end result has restored The Lane to its position as the finest historic theatre in Britain, and gives a new generation of audiences the best experience of any theatre in the West End.

The auditorium was gutted as part of the huge restoration project.

Before and after: the Foyer.

61

The £60m restoration project employed more than 300 building specialists at one time or another, responsible for every stage of the project, from pouring concrete on the ground floor to gilding the roof.

Ian Cairnie's grisailles

The fourth Theatre Royal in Drury Lane opened to the public in 1812 as London was mesmerised by the arrival of the Elgin Marbles at the British Museum. Architects wanted to echo the great stone reliefs in their architecture. Six huge recesses on the stairs were probably originally intended for *trompe-l'oeil* panels depicting Greek figures as at the British Museum. In 2017 Andrew Lloyd Webber commissioned the painter Ian Cairnie to paint six canvases to fill these spaces in three-dimensional grisaille (grey-scale painting). The subjects are not Greek gods but famous musicals that ran in the theatre, including *My Fair Lady* and *Show Boat*. One painting shows Andrew Lloyd Webber meeting the brilliant musical duo Rodgers and Hammerstein.

Craft at The Lane

Every element of the restoration project was planned in meticulous detail, from the painting of a new front cloth for the fire safety curtain, reproducing previous safety curtain designs, to the metal details on the uniforms worn by the Red Coats, the front-of-house staff, to the cocktails served in the Cecil Beaton Bar. A team of craft specialists was employed to recreate the splendour of Wyatt's original Georgian theatre and no detail was too small to be researched and considered: the exact shade of paint used in the Rotunda and staircases; the lavish decorative plasterwork and gilding; the decoration on the crockery used in the Grand Saloon.

The furniture in the Foyer, specially commissioned from cabinet maker Mark Stephens, was made from a number of magnificent mahogany trees that had been felled in a storm a decade ago and were shipped over from St Nicholas's Abbey in Barbados by the Lloyd Webbers. Tragically, elements of the commission were destroyed in a warehouse fire the day before it was due to be shipped and had to be entirely remade less than two months before the reopening.

The front cloth of the fire safety curtain was hand-painted by scenic artists Chris and Liz Clark.

The crockery in the Grand Saloon was specially commissioned from Kit and Minnie Kemp.

OPPOSITE Work on the auditorium ceiling decorations and gilding was carried out by specialist decorators Campbell Smith.

Hand-painting the plasterwork.

Final touches on the statue plinths in the Lower Rotunda.

The specialist plasterwork was carried out by Stevensons of Norwich.

The bespoke furniture in the Foyer was made from mahogany trees felled in a storm and shipped from Barbados.

Afternoon tea is now served in the splendour of the Grand Saloon.

A Theatre for the 21st Century

The day after *42nd Street* closed in October 2019, work began to restore the front-of-house area to its original Georgian glory and to make the oldest theatre in London a fitting centrepiece of Covent Garden. A street café, restaurant and shop welcome the public throughout the day while the early-20th-century auditorium has been reconfigured with new seating tiers that create a flexible space and allow the audience a more intense connection with the performance on stage.

For more than a century The Lane has been home to the spectacular. Its mighty stage and advanced technology have made possible what often appeared to the audience as impossible. At the same time the theatre has set the standard for musical theatre with a string of famous and often record-breaking productions. New life injected into the theatre by the major restoration completed in 2021 sees The Lane set for another century of mind-blowing nights out.

Ever since Thomas Killigrew opened a theatre on this site more than 350 years ago, the Theatre Royal Drury Lane has been entertaining and inspiring audiences.

The restoration complete, The Lane can take its place once more at the heart of entertainment in London, one of theatre's greatest stars reborn.

The Garden is a relaxed café and bar.

This edition © Scala Arts & Heritage Publishers Ltd, 2023
Text by Pamela Hartshorne © LW Theatres, 2023

First published in 2023 by
Scala Arts & Heritage Publishers, 305 Access House, 141–157
Acre Lane, London SW2 5UA. www.scalapublishers.com
In association with LW Theatres

ISBN 978-1-78551-398-5

Printed in China   10 9 8 7 6 5 4 3 2 1